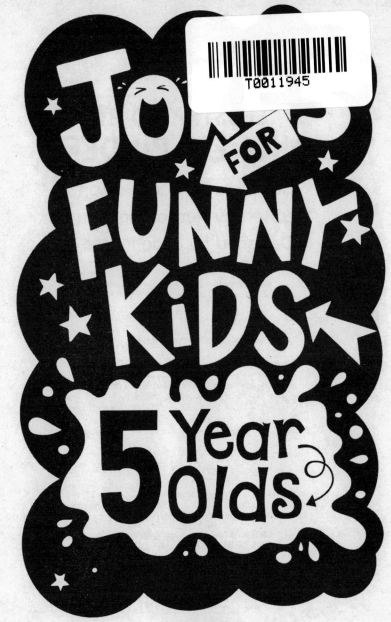

JOKES FOR FUNNY KIDS

5 Year Olds

BUSTER BOOKS

ILLUSTRATED BY
ANDREW PINDER

Compiled by Gary Panton
Edited by Hannah Daffern
Designed by Jade Moore

First published in Great Britain in 2023 by Buster Books,
an imprint of Michael O'Mara Books Limited,
9 Lion Yard, Tremadoc Road, London SW4 7NQ

W www.mombooks.com/buster f Buster Books 🐦 @BusterBooks 📷 @buster_books

A CIP catalogue record for this book is available from the British Library.

ISBN: 978-1-78055-963-6

1 3 5 7 9 10 8 6 4 2

This product is made of material from well-managed, FSC®-certified
forests and other controlled sources. The manufacturing processes
conform to the environmental regulations of the country of origin.

This book was printed in August 2023 by
CPI Group (UK) Ltd, Croydon, CR0 4YY.

FSC
MIX
Paper | Supporting
responsible forestry
FSC® C171272
www.fsc.org

CONTENTS

Doctor, Doctor!	5
Knock, Knock!	18
Animal Antics	31
Dippy Dinosaurs	43
Under the Sea	56
Silly Spooky	69
Funny Food	82
Giggles on the Go!	94
Out of this World	106
Yuck!	117

INTRODUCTION

WHAT DO DOGS LIKE ON THEIR PIZZA?

Pup-eroni.

Welcome to this super-silly collection of the best jokes for 5-year-olds.

In this book you will find over 150 jokes designed to make you roll on the floor laughing, from classic Doctor, Doctor and Knock, Knocks, to dippy dinosaurs, funny food and even giggles on the go!

Don't forget to share the jokes you like the most with your friends and family and give everyone a serious case of the giggles!

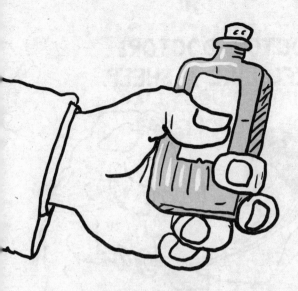

DOCTOR, DOCTOR!

DOCTOR, DOCTOR!
I FEEL LIKE A SHEEP.

Oh no, that sounds

BAAAAAAAAAAD.

DOCTOR, DOCTOR! I KEEP HEARING A RINGING SOUND.

Then answer the phone!

DOCTOR, DOCTOR! EVERYONE THINKS I MAKE THINGS UP.

I don't believe you!

DOCTOR, DOCTOR! I ONLY HAVE 59 SECONDS TO LIVE!

I'll be with you in a minute.

DOCTOR, DOCTOR!
I FEEL LIKE I'M INVISIBLE.

Who said that?

DOCTOR, DOCTOR! I GET A BURNING FEELING EVERY TIME I EAT BIRTHDAY CAKE.

Take the candles
off next time.

DOCTOR, DOCTOR!
I HAVE A STRAWBERRY
STUCK UP MY NOSE.

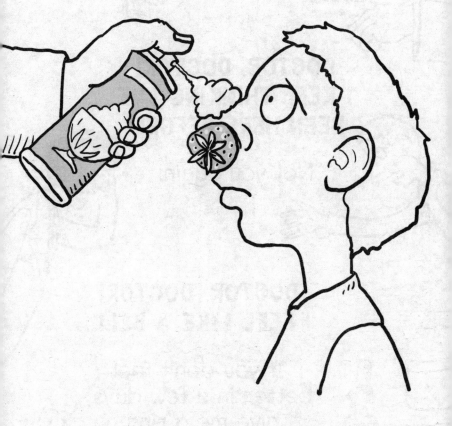

I'll give you some
cream for that.

DOCTOR, DOCTOR! I FEEL LIKE A BEE.

Buzzzzzz off!

DOCTOR, DOCTOR! I KEEP THINKING I'VE BEEN HERE BEFORE.

Not you again!

DOCTOR, DOCTOR! I FEEL LIKE A BELL.

If you don't feel better in a few days, give me a ring.

DOCTOR, DOCTOR! EVERYONE KEEPS IGNORING ME.

Next, please!

DOCTOR, DOCTOR! EVERY TIME I DRINK A MUG OF HOT CHOCOLATE I GET A PAIN IN MY EYE.

Try taking the spoon out first.

DOCTOR, DOCTOR! I KEEP THINKING THERE ARE TWO OF ME.

One at a time, please.

DOCTOR, DOCTOR!
CAN YOU HELP ME OUT?

Of course, just go out
the way you came in.

DOCTOR, DOCTOR!
I FEEL LIKE A BIN.

Don't talk rubbish.

DOCTOR, DOCTOR!
I FEEL LIKE A CARROT.

Don't get yourself in a stew.

KNOCK, KNOCK!

Who's there?

ATCH.

Atch, who?

BLESS YOU!

KNOCK, KNOCK!

Who's there?

BOO.

Boo, who?

WHY ARE YOU CRYING?

KNOCK, KNOCK!

Who's there?

LETTUCE.

Lettuce, who?

LETTUCE IN, IT'S FREEZING OUT HERE!

KNOCK, KNOCK!

Who's there?

ICE CREAM.

Ice cream, who?

ICE CREAM SO YOU CAN HEAR ME.

KNOCK, KNOCK!

Who's there?

WATER.

Water, who?

WATER YOU ASKING SO MANY QUESTIONS FOR? JUST OPEN THE DOOR!

KNOCK, KNOCK!

Who's there?

OWLS GO.

Owls go, who?

YES, THEY DO!

KNOCK, KNOCK!

Who's there?

CAR GO.

Car go, who?

NO, CAR GO BEEP BEEP!

KNOCK, KNOCK!

Who's there?

MARY.

Mary, who?

MARY CHRISTMAS AND A HAPPY NEW YEAR!

KNOCK, KNOCK!

Who's there?

SMELL MOP.

Smell mop, who?

SMELL YOUR POO?
NO WAY!

KNOCK, KNOCK!

Who's there?

I ATE MAP.

I ate map, who?

YUCK!
YOU ATE YOUR POO?

KNOCK, KNOCK!

Who's there?

ABBY.

Abby, who?

ABBY BIRTHDAY TO YOU!

KNOCK, KNOCK!

Who's there?

COWS GO.

Cows go, who?

NO, SILLY, COWS GO MOO!

KNOCK, KNOCK!

Who's there?

SNOW.

Snow, who?

SNOWBODY BUT ME.

KNOCK, KNOCK!

Who's there?

JUSTIN.

Justin, who?

JUSTIN TIME FOR CAKE.

KNOCK, KNOCK!

Who's there?

ANNIE.

Annie, who?

ANNIE-BODY HOME?

ANIMAL ANTICS

WHAT'S ORANGE AND SOUNDS LIKE A PARROT?

A carrot.

WHERE DO COWS GO ON A SATURDAY NIGHT?

To the mooooo-vies.

WHAT DO YOU SAY WHEN A COW'S IN YOUR WAY?

MOOOOOOOOOVE!

WHY DO BEES HAVE STICKY HAIR?

Because they use
a honey-comb.

WHY DO GIRAFFES HAVE SUCH LONG NECKS?

Because they have smelly feet.

HOW DO PIGS SAY HELLO?

With hogs and kisses.

HOW DO YOU START A BEAR RACE?

Ready, teddy, go!

WHAT DO YOU CALL A DANCING COW?

A milkshake.

WHAT'S THE DIFFERENCE BETWEEN ELEPHANTS AND BANANAS?

Bananas are yellow.

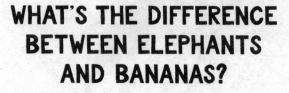

WHAT DO YOU GET IF YOU CROSS A SHEEP WITH A KANGAROO?

A woolly jumper.

WHAT DO YOU CALL A MONKEY IN THE NORTH POLE?

Lost.

WHAT DO YOU CALL A HORSE WHO LIVES NEXT DOOR?

A NEEEEIIIGGGHHHH-bour.

WHERE DO SHEEP WASH?

In the BAAAAAA-th.

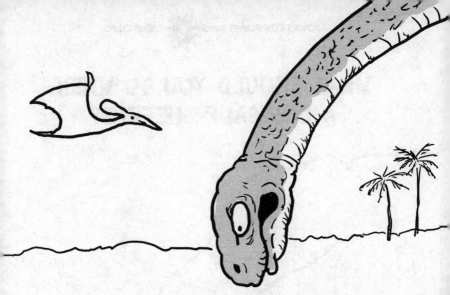

DIPPY DINOSAURS

WHAT SHOULD YOU DO WHEN A DINOSAUR SNEEZES?

WHAT DO YOU CALL A DINOSAUR THAT DOESN'T WASH?

A stinky-saurus.

WHAT DINOSAUR HAS TO WEAR GLASSES?

Tyrannosaurus specs.

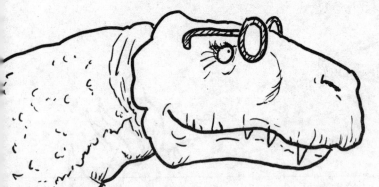

WHAT DO YOU CALL A BLIND DINOSAUR?

Do-you-think-he-saurus.

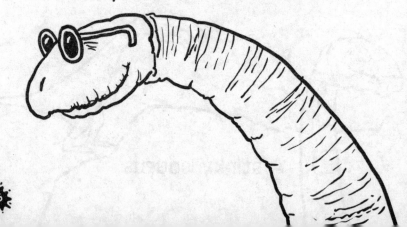

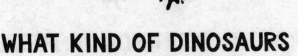

WHAT KIND OF DINOSAURS JOIN THE POLICE?

Tricera-cops.

HOW DO YOU KNOW IF THERE'S A DINOSAUR UNDER YOUR BED?

Your nose is squashed
against the ceiling.

HOW DO YOU KNOW IF THERE'S A DINOSAUR IN THE FRIDGE?

The door won't shut.

WHAT DO YOU CALL A T. REX THAT LOVES CHRISTMAS?

A tree rex.

WHAT DO YOU CALL A BABY T. REX?

A wee rex.

WHAT DO YOU CALL A T. REX THAT NEEDS THE TOILET?

A pee rex.

WHAT SHOULD YOU DO IF YOU SEE A T. REX?

Hope it doesn't see you.

WHAT DO YOU CALL A SLEEPING DINOSAUR?

A Tyranno-snore-us.

WHAT DO YOU GET WHEN A DINOSAUR WALKS ACROSS A STRAWBERRY FIELD?

Strawberry jam.

WHAT DO YOU GET WHEN A T. REX CRASHES ITS CAR?

A Tyrannosaurus wreck.

WHY DID THE T. REX
EAT RAW MEAT?

Because barbecues
hadn't been invented yet.

UNDER THE SEA

WHAT DO SEA MONSTERS EAT?

Fish and ships.

WHICH LETTER DO PIRATES LIKE BEST?

ARRRRRR!

HOW DOES THE SEA SAY HELLO?

It waves.

WHERE DO FISH SAVE THEIR MONEY?

In the river bank.

WHAT'S THE MOST EXPENSIVE FISH?

A goldfish.

WHAT KIND OF FISH COMES FROM OUTER SPACE?

A starfish.

HOW DO YOU MAKE AN OCTOPUS LAUGH?

With ten-tickles.

WHY DID THE SAND BLUSH?

Because the seaweed.

WHY DID THE CRAB GO TO JAIL?

Because he kept pinching things.

WHAT'S YELLOW AND DANGEROUS?

Shark-infested custard.

WHAT DO YOU ALWAYS FIND NEXT TO A JELLYFISH?

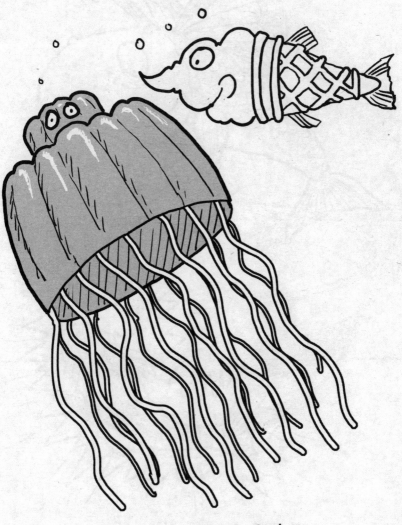

An ice-cream fish.

WHO GRANTS WISHES FOR FISH?

The fairy codmother.

WHAT DO TURTLES DO ON THEIR BIRTHDAYS?

Shell-ebrate!

WHERE DO FISH GO ON THEIR HOLIDAYS?

Fin-land.

WHAT DO YOU GET IF YOU CROSS A FISH WITH AN ELEPHANT?

Swimming trunks.

WHICH DESSERT DO GHOSTS LIKE BEST?

I scream!

WHAT'S THE SCARIEST PLANT?

Bam-BOO!

WHY DO WITCHES ALL DRESS THE SAME?

So you can't tell
which witch is which.

WHAT INSTRUMENT DO SKELETONS PLAY?

Trom-bones.

WHAT DID THE GHOST ORDER FROM THE RESTAURANT?

Spook-etti.

WHAT GAME DO GHOSTS LIKE TO PLAY?

Hide and shriek.

WHO WAS THE BEST DANCER AT THE MONSTER PARTY?

The boogie-man.

WHAT KIND OF WITCH CAN YOU FIND AT THE BEACH?

A sand-witch.

WHY COULDN'T THE SKELETON GO TO THE PARTY?

He had no-body to go with.

WHAT GOES 'HA HA HA' THUD?

A monster laughing its head off.

WHAT TYPE OF FRUIT DO VAMPIRES LIKE TO EAT?

Neck-tarines.

WHERE DO VAMPIRES KEEP THEIR MONEY?

In the blood bank.

WHAT'S BIG, SCARY AND HAS TWO WHEELS?

A monster riding a bicycle.

WHICH SCHOOL LESSON ARE WITCHES REALLY GOOD AT?

Spelling.

HOW DOES A GHOST SNEEZE?

Ah ... ahh ... ahh ... BOO!

WHAT DOES A GHOST WEAR TO HELP THEM SEE BETTER?

Spook-tacles.

FUNNY FOOD

WHAT'S BROWN AND HAIRY AND WEARS SUNGLASSES?

A coconut on the beach.

HOW DO BANANAS SAY THANK YOU?

Thanks a bunch!

WHAT FLIES THROUGH THE SKY AND WOBBLES?

A jelly-copter.

WHY DID THE BANANA GO TO THE DOCTOR?

Because it wasn't peeling well.

WHAT DO YOU GET IF YOU THROW BUTTER UP IN THE AIR?

A butter-fly.

WHAT DID THE EGGS SAY TO THE HEN?

You crack me up.

WHAT KIND OF FLOWERS SHOULD YOU NEVER GIVE ON VALENTINE'S DAY?

Cauliflowers.

WHICH DAY DO POTATOES HATE THE MOST?

Fry-day.

WHAT SNACK MAKES YOU JUMP?

POP-corn.

WHAT'S RED AND GOES UP AND DOWN?

A tomato on a trampoline.

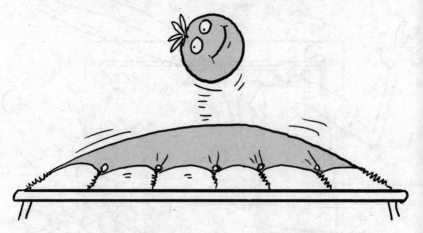

WHAT DID THE MUM TOMATO SAY TO THE BABY TOMATO?

Come on, ketch-up!

WHAT'S GREEN AND GOES UP AND DOWN?

A grape in a lift.

WHAT DO YOU CALL A PAIR OF SHOES MADE FROM BANANAS?

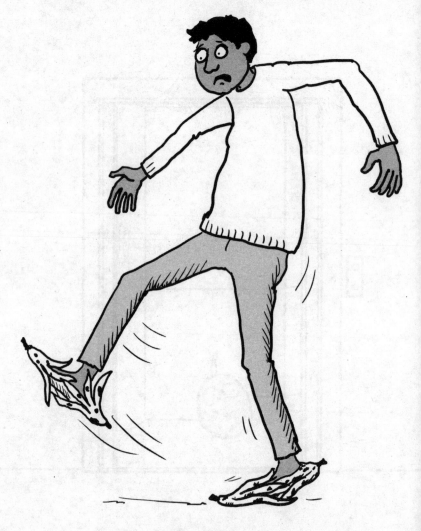

Slippers.

WHAT KIND OF TABLE CAN YOU EAT?

A vege-table.

WHAT'S BROWN AND SQUIRTS JAM AT YOU?

A mouse eating a doughnut.

GIGGLES ON THE GO!

WHAT'S THE DIFFERENCE BETWEEN A CAR AND A DRAGON?

A car only has one horn.

HOW DO YOU FIND A MISSING TRAIN?

Follow the tracks.

WHAT DO YOU CALL A TRAIN FULL OF BUBBLE GUM?

A chew chew train.

WHAT HAS FOUR WHEELS AND FLIES?

A waste disposal truck.

WHAT DO YOU CALL A SLEEPING BULL?

A bull-dozer.

WHAT DO YOU CALL A SNAIL ON A SHIP?

A snailor.

WHY ARE ROADS ALWAYS ANGRY?

Because people keep crossing them.

HOW DO YOU GET TO TOOTH ISLAND?

Take the tooth ferry.

WHAT NOISE DOES A WITCH'S CAR MAKE?

BROOM! BROOM!

WHAT DO YOU SAY TO A FROG WHO NEEDS A LIFT HOME?

Hop in!

WHY DID THE MERMAID BLUSH?

She saw the ship's bottom.

WHAT HAPPENED TO THE WOODEN CAR?

It wooden go.

WHERE DO DOGS PARK THEIR CARS?

In the car bark.

OUT OF
THIS WORLD

WHAT KIND OF PLATES DO THEY USE ON MARS?

Flying saucers.

WHAT SHOULD YOU SAY IF YOU MEET A THREE-HEADED ALIEN?

Hello, hello, hello.

HOW DO YOU THROW A PARTY ON VENUS?

You plan-et.

WHAT DO YOU CALL A PEANUT IN SPACE?

An astro-nut.

WHICH PLANET HAS THE BEST MUSIC?

Nep-tune.

WHICH MEAL OF THE DAY DO ASTRONAUTS LOOK FORWARD TO?

Launch.

HOW DO YOU GET A BABY ASTRONAUT TO SLEEP?

You rock-et.

HOW DO YOU KNOW WHEN THE MOON HAS HAD ENOUGH TO EAT?

It's a full Moon.

WHAT TYPE OF FOOD DO MARTIANS LOVE TO EAT?

Mars-mallows.

WHY DID THE COW GO TO SPACE?

To visit the Moooooon.

HOW DO ALIENS KEEP THEIR SHORTS UP?

With an asteroid belt.

WHAT DO YOU CALL AN ALIEN WITH SIX EYES?

An aliiiiiien.

WHY DID THE SUN GO TO SCHOOL?

To get brighter.

WHY DID THE COW BECOME AN ASTRONAUT?

She wanted to see the Milky Way.

WHICH CHOCOLATE BAR DO ASTRONAUTS LIKE TO EAT?

A Galaxy bar.

WHY IS SNEEZING SO FUNNY?

It's snot.

WHAT KIND OF POO HAS THE BEST SMELL?

Sham-poo.

WHAT DID THE NOSE SAY
TO THE FINGER?

Quit picking on me!

WHY DO GORILLAS HAVE SUCH BIG FINGERS?

Because they have big nostrils!

WHY DID TIGGER STICK HIS HEAD DOWN THE TOILET?

He was looking for Pooh.

WHAT DO YOU CALL A DOG IN YOUR TOILET?

A poo-dle.

WHAT KIND OF BUTTON WON'T UNDO?

A belly button.

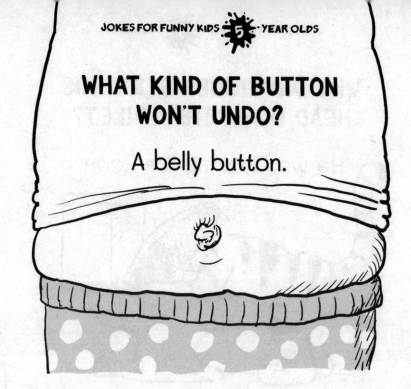

WHY DID THE BOY BRING TOILET ROLL TO THE PARTY?

Because he was a party pooper.

WHAT'S BROWN AND STICKY?

A stick.

WHY DOES NO ONE LIKE POO JOKES?

Because they stink.

WHAT'S BROWN AND SOUNDS LIKE A BELL?

DUNG!

WHY DID THE TOILET PAPER ROLL DOWN THE HILL?

To get to the bottom.

WHAT'S STRONG AND SMELLY?

A stinky cheese lifting weights.

WHAT SHOULD YOU DO IF YOU FIND A BEAR IN THE TOILET?

Let it finish.

WHAT DO YOU CALL AN IGLOO WITHOUT A LOO?

An ig.

WHAT SHOULD YOU DO IF YOUR NOSE IS RUNNING?

Chase after it.

ALSO AVAILABLE: